The Constant Hum of Elsewhere

Cover art: Author, "Ranunculus in Blue"
Cover design: Bri Chapman
Interior design: Bri Chapman
Editor: Allison Blevins
Publisher: Allison Blevins
Executive Editor: Kristiane Weeks-Rogers
Managing Editor: Bianca Dagostino

THE CONSTANT HUM OF ELSEWHERE
JEN ROUSE
ISBN 978-1-957248-59-2
Harbor Editions,
an imprint of Small Harbor Publishing

The Constant Hum of Elsewhere

Jen Rouse

Harbor Editions
Small Harbor Publishing

Contents

The Constant Hum of Elsewhere

I

When You Go to Mardi Gras with Anne Sexton

In New Orleans you flash
your tits and call me *chère*.
You snake your way through
Bourbon Street as though
you are the parade. One of you
is pissing on the sidewalk,
another flinging beads from a float.
For fun you buy a set of crystal fangs
and sneak up to the Carter's balcony.
You bring my wrist to your mouth—
the skin is thin and already scarred
there. You trace my veins with your
tongue and hiss: *this is what
my god wants.*

When I was 14, I recognized in you
the same black heart. The flash
and burn of a brain on fire. I wanted
to know how there could be more
than one of us. But now, dear
succubus, as I watch the blood rise
in your eyes, your pulse pull
against the cords of your neck,
I would give us back. To the concrete
and confetti. To the danger and
the flame. Blow out this candle,
you fucking wretched vampire,
I am already drained.

Somewhere in that Process Lies the Evolution of the Mind

But wait, you are mostly still morons—shouting into the void
like jellyfish first firing their flickering orbs, developing
a sincere and combative sting, those
700 million years ago.

Let me give you the reason for *build*
For *nervous system*   For *brain*

= something mattered/matters/will matter.

Some of you live in the murky depths of *receptive*
and others in the aquatic chemistry of *action*.

Between *think* and *do*, this arc,
this in between. Call it a maze,
call it a network of currents running hell bent,
call it the slow sardonic wit
you wait for when you've gotten
lost in your own ways of forgetting
I exist. You only hear the words when
they collect themselves in brilliant displays,
drawn to the desire to show themselves
to like selves, determined. Yes, you become
determined. You are certain you are
vibrant and worthy. You begin to
learn the language of *react*.

I am the constant reminder
that something has to matter,
that you will never quite walk
on water. Without me.

A Few Words from the Tired Magician

You have sawed me in half
and disappeared me from just
about everything–the swaying
roof of a skyscraper, the bowels
of a submarine, a murky
goldfish bowl, six feet
of brilliant soil, a tomb and
a tightrope and a ticking
bomb. The once beloved
palm of your hand.   Good
lord, the list.

But here's my little secret:
I am terrified of drowning and
my inability to stay out of
straightjackets. This is a kind
of crazy that surfaces like the
mirrored sheen of a dolphin
and disappears just as quickly.
Right as you catch a glimpse of me
going under, I will have already
turned away, turned the disco
ball on, turned the attention
to you. And you are infinitely
flattered. You are spectacular
in the light.

These are choices,
I realize: to walk again into
the water, to allow your
arms around my body in a death
grip, to chain my arms against
your chest, to dislocate us in
an empty attempt at escape. To fill
the pockets with the most
beautiful stones, so what we
say does not matter, just
the secure cinching of the straps,
the body dragging the bottom,
bumping along the sand. Let's

be serious for once and wrap
this up. I am hardly here
already.   My beloved assistant,
my dear executioner.

Remedy

Once there was a clementine
when I couldn't speak

and a late afternoon on
the steps in the sun when

all I could do was think about
your hands so close to my hands.

And sometimes your voice
when no other voice mattered.

Some days we told stories
in sand and each granule was

a day I might put next to another
day until it didn't feel so much

like trying. Now every day
feels so much like trying.

When we first met, you said,
Why not get well?

And I believed you.
And then I didn't.

I woke up in the back of a car,
curled like a nautilus, the sound

of the sea ricocheting inside
my skull.   But I was not an ocean.

I woke up in a cornfield and
the stars pleaded my defense,

but I was not a constellation
or a wanted galaxy. I woke up

in a hotel room, drenched

from days of pulled blinds

and constant doses I forgot to name,
as my own name slipped away.

I woke up and tried to go home.

But I wasn't available.

And neither was home.

I woke up and heard you say
that I couldn't possibly matter enough.

And I remembered then how important
it would always be to remain quiet.

I woke up and wrote every lie
I had ever been told. About god

and hope and the love of someone
coming to sit next to you

when you couldn't be more alone.
I woke up and walked away.

Because no one holds your hair back
when you are fresh out of brilliance.

Because there is no well.
Only *different*.

Remains of the Day

To watch as though from the back
of my being the jobs I have given
my mind—how she loops and
lingers and dwells and dives.
She's kind of like a pelican.

I have a new therapist.
She's kind of like a sandpiper,
hopping along, picking at me
with her tiny beak.   She pulls
out the same chart every week
and classifies me as a manager
and sometimes a firefighter.

This pelican, she is problematic
like that. One minute she's
killing her young, then plucking at her
breast in great sacrifice, reviving
them with her own blood. The next
she's an uncontrollable glutton,
ravenous and slashing into the
sea, collecting her enemies
in her ancient pouch.

On my way out the door,
the new therapist hands me
the bouquet of daffodils
from her desk. She is not
the first therapist to have
done this. I am not sure
why I am always caught
off guard by kindness.

The pelican is so wild
in her heart and mercilessly
headstrong. I breathe her
in and her envious scream rolls
across every synapse, as I choose
other, smaller birds.

Blue Riding Hood

Eventually the wolf
was her grief and she
kept opening the door
to find fierce and ominous
teeth in her grandmother's
clothing. Other days,
six coyotes circled
her in the woods—
her blue cloak and graying
temples. Her hands kept
shaking. She tried to be
still. She lit
signal fires and howled
at merciless stars.   What
big eyes you have, all twelve
of them. And why do they
snarl?   She decided
to name the chupacabras
and pack them gently in her
pickup. She realized
everyone was out to get them
and weren't they just
doing their best to be
magical beasts,
to heal themselves,
to remain
a mystery?

Confession

The beauty of being
bat-shit insane
is that I don't get worked up
about things like weather–
the absence of bread in a snowstorm
doesn't really propel me
towards panic. Or sticking
the car in a snow bank? Eh.
Rock, reverse, repeat. Here's
the thing: I'm the kind
of crazy who does everything
right. You would want me
around in a disaster. I'm a pro
at crowd negotiation, death-
bed vigils, bleeding hearts and
broken children. I will bring
you booze and braid
your hair. I secretly look
for the good everywhere
and often find the fragile.
If you are content, this
crazy wonders: are you
asking the right questions?
Sometimes the bravest
and most ridiculous thing
I do each day is stay
alive.

Spilled

Blood blooms like a poppy
from the bottom of my foot,
but not really like
a bloom or a poppy,
I guess. More like
I-can't-afford-to-lose-it blood–
it looks like watercolors
or kool aid. Not thick or snake-like
or something resembling the word
rivulet. It does not look in charge
of me. Why does no one ever
take charge? In a way that means
take care. For a while,
I wonder if it is mine
as it turns Rorschach
on the linoleum, near the cigarette
burns left by a previous tenant.
I think I might be a previous tenant too–
seeping out through the hole
in my foot. I know things are going
the way of sneaky fucking glass
when every encounter
feels like a punishment. Which
sounds, slightly, like someone
is in charge. Maybe there is
a goddess of slights and
annoyances, a super saint
of tiny-wound affliction?
If so, let me show you
my offering. Here, a splatter.
There, a small galaxy
of DNA. Those?
Those are just spaghetti
noodles. We'll go on
with dinner
anyway.

Playing Poker for Lost Souls or Sitting Across from Your Therapist

You call me an insensitive asshole. I panic. What haven't I noticed? I'm not well. It's not my fault. There are no cards. You tell me you don't know how to play, and, yet, you're winning. I make you anxious. I see you sneak a perfectly-postured singer's breath. *I'll see your hurt little girl and raise you a 45-year-old suicide.* Go big or go home. *Do you want to go home?* you sneer. I am clearly wasting your time. And then I'm looking for you everywhere. Running down subway platforms, through thick-bodied trees in a Minnesota forest, so many arms not yours. There is something, so certain there is something, I must say. Your voice echoes in the emptiness: *What do you want to tell me?* I know if I could just speak the right words you would be happy with me. *Happy people*, you say, *try harder.*

If You Give Anne Sexton a Cookie

If you give Anne Sexton
a cookie, she will lick it
and hand it back to you
and ask for gin. If you give
Anne Sexton some gin,
she will curl her lip and
pout for a pretty cup
with ice and tonic. If
you give Anne Sexton her gin
neat and in a jelly glass,
she will write you a poem.
It is your favorite poem, with
a beautiful line about the door
of a lover's being the same
door as yours. If you remind
Anne Sexton that she is a poet,
she will swallow a bottle
of pills and some window
cleaner. When you tell her
she had to have her stomach
pumped, she will ask about the good-
looking doctor. She will make you
laugh in the middle of all that tragedy.
She will crook her finger to
bring you closer. She will run
that finger down the slope
of your lip. She will smile and whisper
with her head against your breast,
"I'm starving, Darling. Bring
me a cookie."

The Failure of the Analytic Third

I call into the sea and wait for you to sing a self back to me. Sometimes poet, or mother to the girl who is always upside down, or the one who will look you dead in the eye for mercy and find only bones. The songs are all in Spanish. About what is lost. The hand scrapes the bottom and sand. You twirl your gown so lovely as a ghost. And your fingers clutch my throat. What you would make of me is never what I would make of you—and together we float facefuckingdown. I am blue and without symbol. You are not my mother and fraught with meaning. Someone will pull you from me and into the light, sputtering and picking seaweed from your teeth. I'll imagine your siren song. I will let it take me under.

A Few Words from Cleopatra's Lover

You trap the sun
in endless Ball jars,
line them up like
tiny souls on
the window sill.

Let me tell you:
I have watched
your hands for
witchcraft, weights
and measures
against my breast.

Twin-flamed
alchemist, I have
risen time and
again to again
with you, clenched
in my fists. The sun.

But palm opened
and released, you
seethe at my desire,
rage until I turn
phosphorescent.

Oh how you forget
so quickly, the perfume
at the nape of
a neck. Come now,
remember: I am always
a chance of a storm.

Broken

Looks back and feels her breath
rend, the wracking sobs you opened
your arms and chest to hold until
she dissolved her suffering. Salt
into water. Blood into love.

Can't find you in a building
full of rooms, though you pass
by her, you stand in every doorway,
your scent trapped in her throat.

Says, look at me, god, please,
look at me, I am worthy
of your attention.
But not her own.

Never meant to need or
want or treasure the small
jars of gifted herbs, your fine-boned
fingers, your thigh-anchored voice.

Made such a mistake
when she wrote the first word.
When she wrote her sadness
against your name.

Cairn

I.

Maybe the portraits. Dark curls at cords of the neck, close. Candelabra. Holy smoke blowing across the bed. Roses of the dead at your lips. I kept the air for you. Watching your messages transfer from hawk to leaf to palm. And palm to kiss. Where you sit for all my days and drifting nights. This time. And next. And next again. Not a spell. Not in the way they mean now. The witches who do not know that what comes next is what remains from a time they never knew. But I do. Remember the ways of passing each breath, here, now and between us. Come. The way you remember all my words. Woman began in my mouth. Not so long ago. And so long ago. You are small to me here. Where we are cold. And the drapes are drawn.

Knocknarea Hill, County Sligo

Just there in the woods. The silky fuzz of your newly shorn head against my breast. So young and smitten. You followed me to the top. And that night, after the bar, so proud, called your fiancée from a phone booth to say: *Maybe her. Just her. Her name?* a whisper.

Ghost girl. Intoxicating. Wild. And the wind on the hill drags at your heels, back. Home. I am queen and queen again. Open into the cry of the lambs on the sea side. We stumble down. Skin knees and cling to burn in the salt and surf. Let me show you how to hold the weight of me. Listen when I tell you: *choose one stone.*

II.

Followed the years of armor. A mesh of sword and anger heft. You met me in every parking lot. Always: *What do you imagine will happen between us?* I lit your Salem. I licked the menthol from your lips. Maybe you held us there, two women on a mountain. Dangerous with swans and poems. But I was so much: *When all is ruin once again.* You were soft and captured

laughter. So many times I begged you to leave. So many times you stood
in my light.

III.

Ames, IA

When he said, *I know, I love her too*. I learned
the art of living from the middle. The constant
cowardice of others. And leaving alone.

IV.

Betrayal and belief will find
you on a grey leather
couch staring down
an aging psychologist, letting
her finger trail your cheek.
Then those long lunches
at the gallery. The Rothko.
The last time when she said,
I didn't realize how beautiful.
                    How damned.
And then a burgundy couch.
And then a couch in garish florals.
And finally a couch, impenetrable
and her dead husband
in the corner of the room,
constantly glaring at you.

V.

Iowa City, IA

Then, there's an ER, alone. Because no matter
how many times you show up, no one
ever accompanies you. Maybe your expectations
are as high as the manic kite you fly. Maybe when
you crumble again, you'll choose not to
eat the crumbs. Choose not to eat their crumbs.

IV.

When you don't sleep for days,
you watch Claire Danes pretend
to bipolar cry. And she tells you,
with a coy side eye, here, this
is what I do:
                    First admit.
It will all rain down upon you
like the crazy it is. Be ready.
Wipe the lens, and slowly knit
your brows in a most deliberate
pout—the one you saved from
childhood, all puff and stomp.
                    Second admit.
Nothing will stop the hand
of god. So learn to run
like a serial killer is behind
you. Hold the scream in
the pocket of your jaw,
the wet sand of it saturated
until the water washes
up through your eye sockets.
                    Third admit.
Betrayal is your most constant
bedfellow. Walk through
it like Athena, each finger of flame
tracing your brain to melt. The slight.
The mishap. The never special.
                    Fourth admit.
You are a terrible, beautiful
force. Flick the granules of
sadness from your lashes
and blink as quickly as possible.
                    Fifth admit.
Every angle is a camera
angle. Flair your nostrils
in abandon. Pretend
bewilderment. Carry the wildness
in your mouth like sacrament.
Grace be. Kneel into it.

Anne Sexton Reminds Us

Let me tell you, I had a very distinct
voice inside me, violet-eyed, named
Elizabeth. We did everything
in front of the cameras. Such
great pharaohs together. All of those
snakes between us. Isn't it so often
about how you choose to hold
one in the end? Let me tell you,

I kissed the last so hard
poison flooded my throat—
from his couch to this coffin.
Only he forgot to leave the flowers,
no sad sad prayer shared between us,
no Antony to my Cleopatra.

Let me tell you, before my death,
they clung to me like desperate
fans to their starlet. They kept
constant track, sweet
little mice, of my drinking and
my sadness. Only other women
will do that. Whether or not
I answered the phone was
their constant companion. Sometimes,
when I finally took a call, I'd say:
O Sillies, let me tell you,
you simply have to look for me
a little longer, a little harder,
with all of your hands, with all of
your forgiveness. I am always. Your Anne.

II

The Constant Hum of Elsewhere

You should busy me.
Make sure I have something to do
with my hands. Give me manicured
lawns and lovely buildings,
all of these combined provide
"a special apparatus for
the care of lunacy."[1]

In case you were wondering, I have never
been admitted. Never quite the right fit
for here or there. Even my doctors
are uncertain: *Swallow the blue pill*
or don't. Call me
but I won't answer. I will keep you
and then throw you away.
Against that wall, throw yourself
against that wall. It's not so hard
when you just try to focus
on the good things.

I like flamingo croquet
and painting tea cups. I am not
a very good listener, distracted,
as I am, by the constant hum
of elsewhere.

---

[1] Psychiatric Services. "The Kirkbride Plan: Architecture for a Treatment System That Changed." 27(7). 1976.

Gone

There is a table. A sweating glass.
And your hands. Here is a table.
A town. A home. My hands.
Bound. Here is where I heard
you laugh for the first time. Or
the millionth. It rings the same
in this tower. This town. Inside
the bells of belief, I listened
from across a table. A glass.
An hour. —and I have taken
a lover. A town. A home. Not
my own. Not you. Or yours.
I have taken a handful of sunsets.
And turned them over my tongue.
Like your laughter. There has never
been. Ours. I went inside and slowly
turned around the tower. All glass.
The crack was imperceptible. The imperfection
was so small and rooted. I touched
the town. Untouched your hands.
Unbound belief. The glass. An hour.
There is a table. Your laughter.
Someone else will remember.
It will not be me.

Riding with Anne Sexton

I.

I am hungry to sit beside you in your cherry red Mercury, carving my body into the leather, curling into your mother's fur coat like your kitten. I want you with a hunger so ancient it is without a tongue. The drape of your leg and thigh exposed to my fingers. Touch my fingers to your lips and growl with the engine. Let's go together. Close the garage. I have knelt into your starred sonnets and pulled your delicate pearls through my teeth. You are not forgiven your grave grave perversions or extortions. The grandeur in a rocks glass and eyeballs lolling on fumes. I will not forgive you. The language. The shame. Always at the table of discontent. You taught me to dine on loneliness and parade the brave face, brick after mortared brick. Here we are, darling, in the car. Vodka fresh and radio blaring. I know the bottom of that glass like I know god —and neither ends or begins in me, but I go on and you remain. Cherry red, lipstick-stained cigarette, and your name against my name. *Anne.* And this pain. That curls up on the leather beside you and calls you home.

II.

You picked him up on the side of the road. I was there, in the backseat, and you moved the mirror just so. I closed my eyes and inhaled the menthol stench of your Salem. I inhaled your sickly scent caught like a spider in my hair. I thought I might sleep through it. I thought maybe you'd at least stop at the Rushmore Motel, so I might revisit my youth with a cherry cough syrup chaser while you got a room. I'm so fucking tired of you. And the slapping of skin against vinyl. And now, now as you grunt and buck like you like it. As you pull out your ridiculous lasso. Let me tell you, I will go. Unlock the door. I will decapitate the darkness.

III.
One of us is drunk again,
head wagging out the window,
and screaming into traffic,
Where is the death you promised me?
It's not appropriate,
this behavior at this age at this point
in a world in crisis. But we've never
been appropriate. We make a stop
at the 7-Eleven for Slim Jims.
You cry in the toilet for an hour.
They kick me out and tell me to take you with me.
Of course, of course, I have to take you with me.
Your mid-century modern is trashed
with vomit. Your hair is matted
and your lipstick smeared into
your cheek. I am all out of pity
and gods to please you with. They
took all the food and fucking
with them anyway. They said, *no,*
really, this is excessive, even
by our standards—and if you think
we're going to open the door
when you knock once more,
you better have a believable story.
I told them I understood.
I told them we'd try harder next time.

Petite Rouge

I.
Not to forget or remember
but to undo. Put me to sleep
like all your fairytale girls.
And while I'm there bumbling
around in my sad nightgown,
unwind your voice from my ear,
your arms from my waist,
that last morsel of cake—poisoned
with shame. It was a long walk
with you lurking behind me in
the forest. There will be brambles
and briars and all sorts of shards.
As I sleep and as you pluck each piece
from my brain, count them all,
and count them back. Curse
as loudly as you want, I won't
hear you. And with each stab
and drip of remorse,
take my hand and take
yourself away.

II.
Now I am famous and
dead. Called Red and
collapsed in the belly
of all beautiful tales.
Immortal and sliced
like slivers of the best
foie gras. I ask you now,
who wouldn't
want me? Want me.

III.
Once upon a time,
I wore all my capes
for you. And with
every turn of the needle,
every small stitch,
I smiled, never realizing

I had linked my love
to thorns, to fangs.
So listen:
for every girl
in love with another,
there is always a wolf

and a dangerous path.
Choose wisely. Or wildly.
Or not at all.

Goddess of the Cornfield

She says in a voice
reminiscent of the rapture:
"It will all happen again,
with or without you."

The new sky emerges
from an open fist of spring.
A statue here in a winter-
torn field, all thigh and calf
planted, she waits
for the dust to stop
its frenzied dance
around her. She is holding
the light, fierce in her belly.
She carries the clouds,
full of bloom, in her wide-
open fingers. Hear the subtle
crack in her smile, slow
to thunder and watercolor
rage. She is all emerging,
golden. She is all falling,
plum-gray crocus. She pretends
at night she doesn't remember
the winter when
she went away. The winter
when you took the light
and turned her under. Thunder
of soil raining
on a grave.

And maybe that is what
it took to wake
her. How the words
brave and shame
split
the last
breath
of air
between
them

and sputtered,
choose.

Commute

Like being in a sepia-
tinted photograph, the edges
crusting, this morning light
settles in like cream through
murky coffee.
A woman on a bicycle
with a tiny dog poking her
head out of a basket
passes. I wait
for things to come out of a wind
like this. Something slightly
acidic rises and the clouds swoop
down like soft vultures.
Windows split into rock candy
crystals. Birds or
children or trains seem
to scream from a distance
that is here. Now. I should
sit up and pay attention,
hands at 10 and 2.
When they find the car,
twisted like a coat hanger,
a few fields over, I should
be ready for a close up--
metal bars and shadows.
Cameras eat this shit up,
and maybe
I'll be blonde
and wrapped in a shower
curtain. Maybe I'll be
the wrong woman.

The Math of Anne Sexton

I am divided. The brazen
and the long-suffering. Mad
and brilliant and ridiculous
and wrong. I am never an
easy equation. Maybe you'll
try to hold my hand during
lunch and I'll let you, only to purge
you from these swollen eye
sockets with sticks and empty
stones. Your words will
always wound me. So come
closer. Or don't come at all—
in this math I never matter.
But I will make you believe
I am a multiplier of souls.

A sum of these parts will
never equal a whole—
of a me,
or a you,
or an us.

Split the petals and make me
your nursery rhyme. Your oxeye
daisy of truth. She loves me.
He loves me not.

I am divided.

Apotropaic

Turn the bowl upside down
and bury your heart
at the threshold.
There are no demons
that are not your very own.
You say, *all women
are sorceresses*—
but only because
you are so easily seduced.

By the time it takes
to bury the bowl
and build this house around it
maybe your faith will
fall down around you,
maybe the demon
you are so hesitant
to embrace will boldly
enter anyway.

What have you scripted
on this earth-darkened rim?
Serpent swallowing
its own tail? A tether
to keep the dead in place? Oh, we have all
been there. Knocking on
our own doors, jumping
at the glimpse
of a reflection
in a corner of the night.

Ride the Snake

In the Valley of Fire, her Mercury
Cougar sighs and purrs one last time,
gives up the ghost. There's just enough
battery power left to blare The Doors
as the heat begins to slither its
way into the open windows. *He's
hell bent on dying, you know? Loves
the Mojave and a good trip.* She
cranks the sound just a little more,
rocks against the leather, silk
headscarf fluttering somehow in
the windless desert scape. She pounds
the steering wheel to the frenetic
drum beats, and drifts into his final
message: *This is the end, beautiful friend*
This is the end, my only friend
The end[2]

Do you ever wonder about these ancient
messages? She's left the car
to trace her hand shakily over a petroglyph.
Unconcerned that we're being whipped
by the tail of a red sandstone serpent.
And all that's in the car is piss-warm
vodka. *Don't you want to throw*
a spear and see what you'd hit? I would
lead the group. I would be the hunter
with the most prowess! Maybe this
is a poem. Maybe they were on a journey
too. Maybe they were just out here
riding the snake. Lucky bastards. I
bet they found god.

It's hard to stop her. I used to say:
"When she's like this." But she's
always like this. Until she's not,
and we curl up in the center

---

2 Morrison, Jim. "The End." The Doors. Elektra, 1967.

of the sidewinder, waiting it out,
or pulling as though one of us
made it to the other side.

Chasing the Dragon

Tell me what
the dormouse said.
Tell me how
a junkie spends
her day. Tell me whatever
was broken
was unnecessary
anyway. Tell me
all you crave now
is quiet. Tell me
how to ride the beast
and wield the sword.
Tell me when you crack
your jaw wide
you don't sing about
forgiveness anymore.
Tell me why it's you
the mirror bleeds
and bleeds for –and
the moon sends
out her light like
a million stallions
galloping. Tell me
how does your god go
down—on a bed of thorns or
crowned?

Undoing: The Book of Being Here

She sheds her cloak her skin her internal organs watch the sinew snap the
jaw gape wide something wild in eye sockets where the rain slithers down
determined cheek bones

Her arms push against the sky and fire folds around her feet floating just
above just enough to know she isn't quite with you anymore

I never meant this living
I never meant this lightly

A small tattoo
A sigh against this skin

If you carve the words in sadness,
know them like the ink you bury,
like the veins that rise to the occasion.
You have done yourself
no favors. Weave each spell
backwards. Feel the soft weight
of the clouds in your chest.
To isolate one emotion,
to learn to say yes to it,
and move on.

For this House to Stand

Here's how this is going to go:
You are going to ask
if you can read me a story. About a carpenter
who has to tear a house down. It will take years
to rebuild the foundation. Because instead
of bricks, she will choose smooth beach stones.
Certain of the sound of waves
and paths of water. The sensuous hands
of the sun. The house will be terrified at first.
Howling with a north wind
through doubtful rafters. Holding tight
to a door that will no longer close. Eventually,
the carpenter will no longer see this house
as one to sell or leave behind. Eventually,
the house will fold itself around the carpenter—
quiet, sound, so certain of her.

Here's how this is going to go:
I'm going to ask you to read a story to me. And I am going to
listen with everything I have, with no howling
or unhinging. Because the sound of you
is necessary. For this house to stand.

Here's how this is going to go:
I am going to tell you a story. About the way
I watched your hands build me back.

A Remarkable Kind of Attention

I.

For every trick
or treater at the
door, I adjust
my height.
I hover
and remark
on a unique
costume detail
with sincere
delight. I believe
there is a kind
of bravery
in asking to be
seen. In asking
to be noticed
as magnificent.

II.

You believe
my favorite
candy type
is histrionic.
It leaves a nice
sour coating
on your tongue—
reminding you,
perhaps, that
on the day
I asked not
to die, you
closed
the door,
that crumpled
wrapper:
HELP ME
twisted, the last
in the bottom

of the bowl.

III.

At the end
of the film,
Ingrid, in her
complete
genius, swears
she is simply
too mad
to save her
once-upon-
a-captor.
Sometimes
you take a knife
and turn your
back. No matter
how beautiful
those arms felt
and felt again
and once again
like ropes
around you.
When you
confuse candy
and safety.
When you
hear: *this
reminded me
of you. But I
never actually
think of you. Because
why, why would
I turn to see
someone
who is always
half in
shadow?*

IV.

The beauty
of knowing
where the
absence of
shimmer shows
a missing scale.
Where the blade
will fall the fastest.
How you will
look back at me
Betrayed. How
you will cringe
at a certain kind
of laughter. Tell me
again, just
how much
you did (trick)
and didn't (treat)
love me.

V.

Let me tell
you, I looked
you in the eye
every single time.
And when I
took your hand
like a delicate piece
of handspun
sugar, I felt
the molten
core of where
you began. And I
ended. A remarkable
kind of attention.

Abjection

In the abject there is no balance.
No meditative state.
No drift or float.
When you make your pain your art your pain your art your pain your art
your pain,
what hangs in the liminal space?
And who will be with you there—if
you aren't a being—
and you
transcend the need
to belong?

They will want to give you clean sheets.
They will want to cauterize
those veins and return
your uterus to its
proper place.
That's what they do.
They will want to medicate you
and
pat your arm.
And they will feel grateful
in the middle of
all that waste,
all that taboo
and exhibit;
they will feel giddy
because the gift
you have given them
is that they are
not you.

Episode

I.
O, I am the show,
bathed in golden light. My followers
at my feet, clawing at the dazzle–
just wanting to be inside
me for a moment,
my scent carved into memory
like cinnamon and shadow. Showing you
how my mouth caresses
greatness, as desire glistens in my teeth
like an old-friend habit
I am certain I keep quitting.
To lessen the craving–for composure is so overrated
and the voices don't really love me
anymore. Their fingers rip at my skull
so wide and deep, the melting
into the gorgeous web
of hemisphere battle.

II.
And every song is on repeat because it is the only order I can tolerate. I
hit the button so hard
I feel like my fingers will crush through the dash. Sunglasses launch
from my hand as though to punctuate the giant fuck you I'm screaming
through the phone, but I'm not really saying fuck you,
no, I am saying I want I need these goddamn corn stalks to stop mocking
me with their blinding
radiance, and I'm saying I need to sleep
and for your voice
just your voice
to sing me somewhere else
because we simply
aren't safe
here anymore.

III.
The mistake in thinking is that there must be some trigger,
something removable or avoidable, a thing that must be healed.
Thorn in paw. If there is a plan…   The mistake in thinking is that
there

is a need to cling to a past way of being, for attention,
for the sake of ritual, for not knowing what else to do.
None of this is true.
I have no desire to be watched or listened to, sought after
or saved. It is not quiet here, clatter of tiles
and words that spell themselves. I am only
as much as you will make of me. Or as little.

Anne Sexton on Baseball

I thought she'd crack a joke
about home runs or the enormity
of a ballpark frank. I thought maybe
she'd turn her cap backwards
and call me babe. Or at least
get smashed and cheer for
the wrong team. I count on her
bad behavior so often, her silence
somewhat threw me.

I took her hand, as I often
do, at great risk of rejection
or irritation. This time she held
on. This time she smiled at me
like she was actually there.
What's wrong? I found myself
softening to her posture, slumped
in the seat beside me. *You know,*
I know everything about you,
nothing you say will shock me.

Yes, well, that's a problem,
isn't it? she belched. *Aren't we*
like them, running the bases
like we'll win? Win some grand prize
at life. A trophy. A moment
of greatness. And all of these
people use them. To get someplace
greater too. Someplace better
than their living room couches. Some
place closer to Baseball Christ.

No matter how many times
you run these bases, I will not love
you. You realize that? The trophy
was always tarnished. You were
never up to bat. Not with me.

Now, find us some peanuts, huh?
And maybe the coach. That's where

this game is going.

End of the World Memory

We sit at coffee discussing
what it means to meet
at abject vulnerability. Everything
catches in my throat, like hearts.

I avoid your hands. The link
that binds my conscious mind
to the mind I might meet
on the other side of the table.

If I have brought you through
from another life, I want
to know why. I don't believe
in cosmic jokes. But I

believe I know you. And if
I brought you here from stars
or seas, I will not leave you.

If the end of the world
plays out in the background,
I will still choose to see only
you, across from me,

our hands tearing into
chests, ripping out those wondrous
hearts, and trading—
to remember when we

can't remember the last
time we met or if I kissed you.

In the Bookstore with Anne Sexton

We sit in the bookstore, watching
the rain roll like waves over the windows.
You are hungry for pie. You are ravenous
here as in all things, licking molten cherry
and bourbon, a crunchy sugar coating,
from your twitching fingers.
Decadent. Debauched. You wear rubies and
buy tomatoes, yes.[3] You linger over covers
and stroke the spines of the titles,
fidgety for a cigarette you're not allowed inside.
You've chosen Maxine's new poems and some
psychiatric hospital history to fumble.   A book
on how to make a superior cocktail.

I watch the rain, unable to concentrate.
I have carried you like a delicate pastry.
You are my elaborate metaphor,
my sometimes touchstone
to a maddening truth. But there is part
of you I will not bury on that beach
you're always rowing toward.
Or explain away. You are the cautionary tale.
A broken egg. A woman who lived like a junkie
on her fame, oozing into madness.
But more often as convenience. How did
you hold a Pulitzer in one hand and
molest your children with the other?
When you threw their dinner
and made them play your mother,
there could've never been a poem
worth that, no matter how it might've
bled through your brain and onto the pillow.

How do you look at me now and pretend
you're not undone? I cannot undo this horrific
part of you, though I've studied your

---

[3] Sexton, Anne. "Rowing." The Awful Rowing Towards God. Boston: Houghton Mifflin, 1975

lines and know what it means to want
a cure, to want a rest. By head. By heart.
When I write your voice, I write into a tide.
When I sit here with you Anne the Gray,
as the rain and the pie melt away, as
the books between us crumble like crust,
I imagine your daughters took some
solace when they heard the words,
ashes to ashes, dust to dust.

Little Conversations

There are no good days.
And though she sometimes
sits beside my bed,
she never takes my hand.
She dangles a leg and hikes
her skirt, drapes a cigarette,
and cocks her head. And cocks
her head, hissing: *dying is an art.*[4]
And, *do it better.* But I couldn't
have carved more signs
in the darkness. I couldn't
have placed the pills
just so or the fifth
of vodka any closer.

She squawks like a drunk parrot: *That's Sylvia's line, not mine, you idiot! Why
do you think you've been stranded?! My god, get your suicides straight!*

Get my suicides straight. Yes. I've had so many. That time the medicine
collapsed
all my thinking and I drove into the sky. And the sky embraced me. And
then the car hit the side of the bridge and there was no sky. Just glass
always glass fine as sand through bloody fingers. Or when the benzos
and the booze make a joyous marriage of blackout in the backseat. Then
there's a street lamp and sobbing. Still there and no way home.

It's how one walks
away in the failure
and lies that wears
one down over time.
I really wasn't trying…
I would never want to…
I am fine. I am fine.
I am fine! What needs
to be heard, obviously,
is that I am fine. That every word
is an elaborate ruse
for attention. Though, sometimes, when

---

[4] Plath, Sylvia. "Lady Lazarus." The Collection Poems. Harper and Row, 1981.

there's a moment of focus,
I raise my head from
the pillow and sneer
back at her, in all her
battered glory: *Boy,
you got me! I truly love
this game.*

III

Inside the Untoward

Here is the edge of beauty and your kiss slides through my hair and into the madness that makes it safe for you to be near me but not near me * and I cannot have this spinning of everything into gold for you no matter how many times I might tell you that I have always known your face, this constant drip of longing * against the tight high wire of tragically bright sun it is so reckless here and your hands a kind of hell fire so that I cannot stand to reach back again but I reach back * again * from that world to this world I find the collapse of kindness unsettling, my inability to say this leaf and this heart are the same so why would you unwind the seasons, why would you untie this sutured space and silence * for god's sake please don't speak! anymore * unless you bring Drano and sit and hold my hand until it ends * until it ends at the edge of beauty and your kiss slides through my hair

Ire of Teeth

I made a dentist appointment. It felt
monumental. Because I hate teeth and
phones and people and calling
and asking for anything and
being reminded that I have teeth
and that they need care.

Because needing feels like teeth clenching.
Because a body feels like waste.

When I ask, "Can you fit me in?"
I am admitting myself for more time here–
and there is already enough drilling:
"Have you cared about every dead or dying thing today?"
Oh, indeed, I have.

There are those who are fortunate enough
to call this: *routine*. They are what I call:
happy. And everything bounces contentedly along
like their ridiculously healthy gums.

In my dreams, teeth are
catastrophic, as are keys.
And losing you.

Birthday Horses

We are approaching 45. It is clipping along
now, stallion-wild, bit clenched and cutting, and words
that roll like cannons into the night. We don't
know what we're shooting at or care if the
angles align. It is time—if there ever has been a time—
for someone to follow. To watch from the woods,
to make gentle fires. She is dancing in the fields again,
the moon at her glossy hooves. They say that
about us, you know, after the galloping, after the
fox abandons the chase and we're still charging
at air. They shake their heads, and mumble   amazing
but were we? Ever? More than a feast for
a ravenous kind of madness?   Were we ever
more than a trick of the light?

Loyal

In the perfect hollow
between cheekbone and jaw,
my thumb caresses
the worn map of your silence.
In this motion of aligning
our foreheads, our never-
tell hearts, what I am saying
is that this illness has carved
itself into 30 years of every synapse,
so don't let go. It's a moment
we never have. And I always have.
It's a pack of cigarettes and a tired
phone call from a parking lot. Because
I am always fleeting. I loose
the world like a hawk unleashes
her sonorous cry. I am not to be admired
or blamed. I do not need a drink
of water or sleep or anything
you would prescribe. I want you
in ways you have never imagined.
Please, trace this shooting star
of sadness across my brain—
let me know all the whorls
of your fingertips, let the touch
of you bring me back. Or let me
go. Please let me go.

Anne Sexton Talks to God

Anne, frantically twisting
her sea-tossed hair through
her fingers: *I'm telling you,*
you see, I've been here
before.   I remember
the way you held me,
and then pushed me
back into the water.
I remember! Why won't
you acknowledge
that I've been here!

God, turned towards
the sunset, back to Anne:
I know. I'm certain,
for you, it felt like that.
For me, it was often you
there, not quite within reach
yet, a tiny bird throwing
herself against the pane
of a window. I wanted
so much for you. But you
wanted your misery
just a little bit more.

Anne, rises from the beach,
throws sand at God–her usual
tantrum: *That's a horrible fucking*
thing for God to say. You're not
really God are you? This is
not where I was supposed
to have landed. Where is my
boat, goddamnit?! I'm going.

God, softly, like the voice,
of an ocean, like the arms
of a tide: *For some of you, I feel*
more maternal, and your struggles
cause me something that manifests
in you as a kind of hellish anguish.

*I would've let you come sooner, but you
were so strong. You had to do
it yourself. Such a constant dervish.
The unsettled rattle of your brain.*

Anne: *You could've saved me.*
God: *You could've saved yourself.*
Anne: *Why am I here?*
God: *You decided to row.*

Under Tongue

Before I go and you refuse
me the prayer of your lips
against mine, let me tell you:
I traced each lineage of herb
to the brain to the tides to
the balance and beyond.
I put the blue pill under my tongue,
the red one above. And cried
at every stoplight. On the night
I sent a message for help
and it said *HELP ME*
you liked something else
on Facebook instead. While I,
I went on dying.

No one who wants to die
will dial a phone number.
All of the words are already gone.
I sat above them—
like a small and insignificant god.
I felt the beauty of the word gone,
and it was cool like the silk
grain of the wood of the desk
against my cheek. And no one
hurt me there or failed
to love me. Because love
is as empty and expansive as
losing the desire to know
what it means to deserve it.

One pill, blue pill. God forgot
to explain the rules pills.

And as that breath slowed
and the body slackened
as though falling into arms
that had not opened,
I was not, and not was more
than what I am now.

In the house of birds

walls quiver with wings.
Her nervous fingers
flutter at her ruby
throat. And every room
has a pedestaled bath,
where delicate finches
dip tiny beaks while
regal hawks hang
from birch chandeliers.
Why am I here, she wonders
again. Her hollow womb,
her spindly ankles? Oh,
yes, of course,
her head. "Hummingbird,"
they said, when she told
them she craved nectar
and couldn't sit still.
"Sanctuary," they said,
when she stopped sleeping
and plucked the feathers
from her crown. It wasn't
this she expected to be.

Not all birds sing
here, she noted.
Some spend all day
constructing meticulous
nests. Others plumping
elaborate plumage.
"Multiple
personalities," hummed
the pigeon, as he hopped
upon her bed.
"Rest,"
she whispered,
but her legs
never
touched
down.

Love's Anatomy

Here is the window—
your breath and back against,
my hand on the glass and longing,
tethered tethered.
There was nothing surreal in our self-portrait
of stars. Fallen. Flooded and spilled
this womb through all our fingers.
I tried so hard to catch you—
stitched and severed—but when I opened
my mouth to scream, only my heart flew out.
A child's balloon. A lost umbilicus.

I will have to walk out of here alone.
I will have to change my name.
Once more I will have to love
something that I will lose.

Tell me again the story of why we are here.
Tell me again the story of hummingbirds and thorns.

And So the Night

I.

I return once more
for the unfurling of sky.
Storms race like dragons
across a fiery landscape,
cracked open like geodes.
No softness in gossamer
shards and pricked fingers.
Their mouths pour rain.
They knock at the window.
The body responds with a desire
to be mythical—beaded
headdress, wings made
of dawn, scepter in
silent orbit. Open
your arms. I am here
beside you.

II.

Her mad chariot rides the night
like I wish she'd ride me—
the rolling thunder of her thighs,
her hair blown back and wild
in the sky. Each word like
hunger, the husky
smoke of manic laughter.
Everyone loves the Artemis-
Mother. Sixty nymphs is
never enough. And I break
open this adoration like a delicate
egg before her.

If You Took Anne Sexton to Costco

Let's just envision for a moment
the Costco. That captivating letter C
shimmering like a scarlet mistress
in the distance, the ultimate promise
of capitalist deliverance. You know you love
that big box store.

Its warehouse ceilings sneering down
and full of fluorescent teeth. Your cart
the size of a slug bug—more! scarlet! You know
the moment by heart, the catch-your-breath-
by-the-big-screens bliss, the way your neck
awe-strains to stare at the monoliths
made of petrified muffins. O yes.

Let's just envision for a moment
one Anne Sexton. One Anne Sexton
walking into the Costco. But she doesn't
just walk. She sashays into the Costco.
She sashays with an old fashioned
and a cigarette and some killer
heels. She definitely calls
it "The Costco." When you're Anne
Sexton, you have to look things
over. There's always a chin up and
down kind of appraisal. Plus
you have to figure out how to push
the cart. When your hands are so
very full. But are we pushing the
cart today? Meh. That's still to be
decided.

Why are we here, again? She looks
me over. She has no idea who I am
or why she'd ever come to such a place.
She takes stock, she passes by a 48-
pack of toilet paper. *I mean, really
darling, who shits this much? This
would last the rest of my lifetime
and, of course, given that short span,*

*probably longer. I'm afraid of disappointing
you, of course, but I can't seem
to remember your name. Or…*

And then, from the corner of her
slightly boozy eyeball, she spots them–
rows and rows, the endless glistening
jewel-hued tones of liquor bottles. *O now,
now, I remember. We must be throwing
a party. Of course. You know I don't
eat when he's gone. You know
I can't host all the friends alone. You
know if the hem of my skirt isn't
straight, I can't sit at the table. You
know, I'm not sure I can do this.
Do you smell that scent? So many
people. Maybe she's here. Nana–
this is where she's gone, right? That's
why you've brought me here?
To the big Costco in the sky?*

She laughs uncontrollably.
She slithers into the cart,
and her skirt catches on a rough edge.
This will end just as you thought
it might. With a mad grab for a bottle
to appease her, some indiscriminate
sobbing—by which one of us may
remain unclear—and we jump the line,
all the lines, but not before we snag
that giant pack of toilet paper, because,
really, really, you just never know.

Pharmakon de Medici

237 cabinets. You are a woman. You are poison. Thorned in this palm, a peony unfurling. When there is a massacre, when the people split and the heavens hide their gods, you refuse to leave the throne. At tea, the devil's trumpet. And all of the ladies unlace. Just a little. There hasn't been a moment for breath. And if they would call you a great king, cunt and all, would you accept the compliment? But they will never. Behind the first door is a pair of perfumed gloves. A fork behind the second. Some science that sounds like sorcery, third. How dare you be Italian. You are a curiosity in your own cupboard. Bad mother. And you are. And you are not. Belladonna. Black widow. When you prick your own finger, what do you taste on your tongue?

Voyeur

And the girl
with the hummingbird head,
well, she was lovely
as a nun, so draped and scaled
and dragon-fiery.
She watched everything
so carefully—
the way the husband and wife
shared a fish in emerald
green. Each bite
caught
in the other's teeth. She thought
it might be romantic
to love a fish so much
and knives and forks.
He was a fork for sure,
pointy and bow-tined. The wife
looked lovely in lemon,
like honey and sun,
running through the hummingbird's
fingers. Wingless. Knife.
Wife. Take
the scarlet heart
and her lips. She turns
her head so quickly
and swears they have
this dinner every night.

Distillation

20 drops per minute. Until the liquid turned vapor leaves a residue so intoxicatingly flammable, everything smells like risk. She said, *let's create a vessel. Let's create an apparatus. Let's slow the process, no need for this hemorrhage of light. We will dissolve, return, split, and form again, with greater intensity. We will not inherit the earth but return to the cosmos. Here you are, my eight-rayed star, my eye in the center of the universe. I will forever rock you in gentle waters.*

But that you won't.

Distill.

To gut oneself of another.   But not completely. Is it possible to mean you differently?

*One becomes two, two becomes three, and out of the third comes the one as the fourth.**

Here is the shadow of longing.

Here is the divine of lost.

* attributed to Mary the Prophetess

Chiromancer

This is the line where I push you away—
see how it breaks and breaks again;
root of the middle finger, Mount of Saturn.
Wisdom in abundance–

or rings full and taciturn?
By now in the reading
I have usually tried
to destroy us at least once.
That double-lined Girdle
of Venus, denoting lust.
Instead, tonight, let
the line of the moon ascend.
Let me linger in your
lace-work skin. Sit beside me,
take my hand.

The Hypatia State

My father said, "You will be
a perfect human." And I
wondered, as a child,
if I was not human,
was I serpent, perhaps?
perhaps circle,
eclipse, or parabola? the curve
of a flat plane cutting
through a cone? Was I,
at all, beautiful? Women,
they said, were not human.
My algebra was different,
but my students never left.

When I would not bend
to bless their christ,
they carved my skin away
with slivers of shell.
They quartered my
body and not for the heavens,
though I knew those heavens
and how they might hold me.
I was an equation
with multiple solutions.
I saw every possibility
in every kind of person,
not just the shapes at
the ends of my fingers--
but the divine forms
transfixed, rooted in
the sight of truth. I chose
to fall in love with wisdom
and reason. I might've
been your perfect human,
I might've been your
philosopher king.

What She Wants to Tell You

There are three things that might save you—
her voice in smoky alto whisper,
her arms stretched, a jurassic wing span,
in a flicker flight of lightning—
and there are three things that won't.
(Insert here a strain of sinister laughter
or three kisses on the top of your head.)
Now make your way home.
I sit on a weeping hill in the rain. I sit beside a sick bed in complete
silence.
I look out onto the orchard. I gather all my strength like apples in a
bucket.
This bucket has a small hole, imperceptible   and the apples
look serene
to anyone who passes. A soul slips through
like liquid silver.   I cup the liquid in thick fingers tight
hand
under
hand.   Each time something else evaporates
I'm guessing at least one of the three things
I need to show you
is gone.
There is silver all over my hands and I am opening them to show how
hard I'm trying.
And when I do this, when I would
announce I have the answer,
my mouth, so desirous,
so eager, is flooded
with
apples.

Who Makes You Feel Safe Will Not be Found

The scream is slow
to form
at my lips—though she
is faceless and
restless, though she
pins me
to the bed and rips
the soul from
my throat. And I watch
myself watch myself
as I suffocate
in her mouth. (I wanted her
mouth to save
me once. At the same time
every Tuesday.)
She swallows me
whole. Huh, I think,
in that unearthly space
where the body slips
from the body, in that
unholy moment
where the undoing
is done, fuck it,
I will not
go this time.

Here is my hand
reaching out from
inside her mouth.
Here is the way
I will pull myself
out and shed
the shell of her.
Here is how I
will take her head
in my hands, her lips
to my lips. Here is how
I will do this, having
always been
done to.

When the Rowing Ended at God

but there will be a door
and I will open it
and I will get rid of the rat inside of me,
the gnawing pestilential rat.
God will take it with his two hands
and embrace it. —Anne Sexton, "Rowing"[5]

In the end, we sat at the worn farm
house table, her manuscript finished.
She'd made her way to an island. Where her
salt-encrusted fingers had rowed
her to some peace. Her sunburned
freckled cheeks luminous
and forgiven. Maybe she didn't
really deserve it, maybe it didn't
matter anymore. The screen door
rocked in a warm wind. She clacked
the final notes on her typewriter keys.

She had long forgotten I was watching,
and so I sat on the beach, sipping tequila.
I mean. I needed to know if the rowing
had been worth it. I'm simply not that work-
brittle. Lessons learned and all that.
We had long been moving between
these worlds. Her death, my life,
the garage and the gas, the line by line,
the therapists and dramatic moments
of collapse. After awhile, it was impossible
to separate the rats from the stars,
the id from the ego from the starving need,
for father, from mother. We ate every amen.

Truthfully, I'm not sure I saw anything,
as she fell from the dilapidated boat
and onto the sand. But her journey had

---

[5] Sexton, Anne. "Rowing." The Awful Rowing Toward God. Boston: Houghton, Mifflin, 1975.

taken so long, and, honestly, no one,
though she had demanded attention,
had bothered to listen. And, so, for one last
time I took her hand. And led her to
an altar of contrition. Dear, Anne,
let me put this holy water to your lips.
Dear Anne, please believe me when I say
that when She held that stunning rat
in her soft, soft hands, I believe
you were delivered.

The Hours that were not Broken

The days string out like honey and sun—
and you grow everything and hold it close
like forgiveness. Like the tender gifts of
beginning again. If I start over.
If you watch and stay rooted. If you/I begin
at what we know. If I begin at less than
risk and abandon. There is nothing of where
we started. There are stars clustered
and ancient. I wanted you to know me.
And how I would never abandon. How I
would throw us out like a net to catch
what is so complicated. How I would throw us out
like a net to catch all of the life we've
wanted. Maybe there is only breath. Maybe
there is the way that I've reached and
you've reached back. Maybe it means
nothing. Maybe it means we are abandoned.
If, however, there is something. We. Pull.
In. If, however, we are not lost to each other.
If I would claim to know you. If you would claim
I never. I still believe in the ways
you have grown here. I believe in the ways you have
shown me this. You. How it shifts and changes
in the light. However you are here.
However I am. These arms fall open.
Again   maybe   again.

Acknowledgements

My thanks to the editors of the following publications, in which these poems first appeared:

The Tishman Review: "Riding with Anne Sexton"
Sinister Wisdom: "Birthday Horses," "Loyal," "Ire of Teeth," and "Inside the Untoward"
Gulf Stream Literary Magazine: "When You Go to Mardi Gras with Anne Sexton," "Anne Sexton on Baseball," and "In the Bookstore with Anne Sexton"
Up the Staircase: "If You Give Anne Sexton a Cookie" and "When the Rowing Ended at God"
the tiny: "The Failure of the Analytic Third" and "The Hours that were not Broken"
Wicked Alice: "What Would Happen if You Took Anne Sexton to Costco"
Midnight Poetry Boutique: "Ride the Snake," "Anne Sexton Reminds Us," "Under Tongue," and "A Few Words from the Tired Magician"
River Heron Review: "Cairn"
Parentheses Journal: "Somewhere in that Process Lies the Evolution of the Mind"
Cleaver Magazine: "Remedy"
The Sandy River Review: "A Few Words from Cleopatra's Lover"
Blanket Sea: "The Constant Hum of Elsewhere"
The Ginger Collect: "Petite Rouge"
Sliver of Stone: "Apotropaic"
The Wardrobe's Best Dressed: "Abjection"
8 Poems: "Episode"
TERSE Journal: "End of the World Memory"
Glass: A Journal of Poetry: "Anne Sexton Talks to God"
Hot Tin Roof, Little Village Magazine: "In the house of birds"
Occulum: "Pharmakon de Medici"
The Feminine Collective: "Distillation" and "The Hypatia State"
MadHat: "What She Wants to Tell You"
The Anatomy of Desire: An Anthology of Distance: "Who Makes You Feel Safe Will Not be Found"

Sincerest thanks to the founders of Headmistress Press for publishing many of these poems in chapbooks: *Acid and Tender, CAKE,* and *Riding with Anne Sexton*. And to Jessica Johanningmeier for all her careful assistance and friendship.

Jen Rouse is the author of *Fragments of V*, *A Trickle of Bloom Becomes You*, *CAKE*, *Acid & Tender*, and *Riding with Anne Sexton*. She Directs Cole Library and the Center for Teaching and Learning at Cornell College.

Advanced Praise

Vulnerable and darkly humorous, Jen Rouse's *The Constant Hum of Elsewhere* flirts with the borders of madness in hallucinatory poems that dote on Anne Sexton, favor the color red, wrangle snakes, wander dream-like landscapes, and interrogate the faith we place in doctors, therapists, and lovers. Claiming the label "crazy," Rouse's speaker fears the unreliability of her own assessments even as she is starved for meaning: "I secretly look / for the good everywhere," she admits, "and often find the fragile." In this book, both the living and the dead inspire ambivalence and awaken desire, becoming mirrors that reflect back the speaker's contradictory relationship to self: "If you are content, this / crazy wonders: are you / asking the right questions?" In these depths, "crazy" is not so crazy after all; the cultural script is flipped. At its core, this book is propelled by brilliant curiosity about what we deem healthy, tracking a mind that refuses a vapid existence or overly simplistic answers.

> Kimberly Ann Priest, winner of the Backwaters Prize in Poetry from the University of Nebraska Press for *Wolves in Shells*

Rather than try to outrun their influences, the oath-shakers, world-shifters, and myth-repairers in Jen Rouse's *The Constant Hum of Elsewhere* invoke their muses without fear. The ensuing dialogues smolder. Who but a poet singing under the star of Anne Sexton could translate "salt into water. / Blood into love"? If ever you have listened to a poem and longed to kiss it on the mouth, this book is waiting for you.

> Joshua Davis, author of *Authentic Embellishments: Fragments of a Life Saved by Poetry*

The Constant Hum of Elsewhere is a collection of many voices that all unite under the singularity of Rouse's poetic voice. Rouse constantly surprises in this book, weaving fairytales and strange creatures into poems that are at once intimate and mythic. Rouse pulls us into scenes of pelicans and coyotes, chupacabras and dragons, succubi and vampires. We also hear from the likes of Cleopatra and Anne Sexton. All of this creates a book with decadently rich imagery, vast metaphors, and twists and turns that will keep you turning the page for more.

> Boston Gordon, author of *Loose Bricks*

About Small Harbor Publishing

Small Harbor Publishing is a 501c3 nonprofit organization. Our goal is to publish unique and diverse voices. We are a feminist press, and we are committed to diversity and inclusion. We strive to bring new voices to a devoted and expanding readership.

Small Harbor Publishing began in 2018 with the first issue of *Harbor Review*. The magazine is an online space where poetry and art converse. *Harbor Review* quickly grew and now publishes reviews and runs multiple micro chapbook competitions, including the Washburn Prize and the Editor's Prize.

In July 2020, Small Harbor Publishing was officially incorporated and began Harbor Editions. Harbor Editions accepts submissions through a chapbook open reading period, a hybrid chapbook open reading period, the Marginalia Series, and the Laureate Prize.

In 2023, Harbor Anthologies began with a mission to promote texts that explore social justice issues and highlight marginalized writers.

If you would like to support Small Harbor Publishing, visit our "About" page at: smallharborpublishing.com/about.